Soul Catcher

LITTLE PIECES OF EVERYDAY WISDOM

THE WRITESPACE BOOKS

ISBN: 978-1-909774-12-4

Published in 2014 by **The WriteSpace – Books**
an imprint of **PubliBook Ireland**
5 Cranbrooke – The Grange – Newcastle Road – Lucan, Co. Dublin, Ireland

A CIP Catalogue record for this book is available from
The British Library and the Irish Copyright Libraries.

Designed, typeset, printed and bound in Ireland by **PubliBook Ireland**

www.publibookireland.com

Soul Catcher

LITTLE PIECES OF EVERYDAY WISDOM

FIONA FAY

Acknowledgments

I want to acknowledge every single person who has dedicated their lives to following their soul. I thank them for their courage, faith and perseverance to listen, despite what the world may have otherwise told them. I also want to thank those who may not totally dedicate their entire lives to this pursuit but who still listen within and even if they do not follow this all the way, they are often led, time to time from this place. Well done to you too!

Dedication

For those who continue to push or struggle and find life difficult. There are other ways to live.

Just as a baby needs love to survive, we too need to love our souls and fill up our inner well. Each day is spent ensuring our bodies are fuelled with adequate food, water, and exercise. We keep our physical needs met and sometimes we forget to tend to our souls.

Introduction

—

This book is a little remedy for your soul. A soul nourishment.

When you nourish your soul and tune into it; it provides a new, vibrant and fresh energy that can cause you to find easier ways to live and a better way to be in the world.

This new approach can cause greater successes in your life and every day miracles, yet so few choose to discover it. Become some of the few that find it and help others to discover it, it will be the greatest gift you will ever receive.

—

Foreword

May this little book nourish you, comfort you and give you a little lift whenever you require it. You are never alone. The universe is always with you and here to tend to your every need and want.

Allow these words to infuse your inner being and reach into the deeper you, where the harmonic sound of the universe beats inside your own heart. It wants you to hear, you are not alone, you have more help than you could possibly imagine.

Enjoy this little journey of soul food, shafts of light, nuggets of inspiration. May it turn your darkest day or hour into a reminder that light is just a breath away.

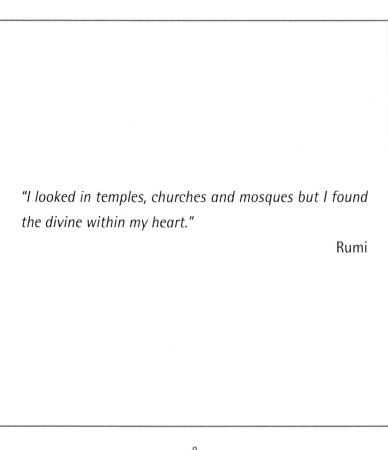

"I looked in temples, churches and mosques but I found the divine within my heart."

Rumi

Soul Catcher

Hello

This is the universe talking directly to you.

You never have to worry again or at least, as much. I am looking after your challenges and your wishes.

From this day forward, you can relax knowing that I am on your side like the most incredible friend you could ask for.

I am always here, listening and dedicated to fulfilling your every request.

You are loved so deeply and held in the highest regard.

Thoughts

Some thoughts make you tired. These are heavy, negative thoughts. Don't listen to them. Watch them pass the window of your mind like snowflakes.

They melt as soon as they hit the pavement. They are nothing to do with you. They are simply snowflakes.

Loving Power

There is a master behind your thoughts. A quietness, gentleness, a loving power, an intelligence.

Your job if you are really smart, is to listen to the master.

Guidance

The master can otherwise be known as the universe, god consciousness, the angels, your inner knowing, your intuition, your gut feeling.

Name this guidance, what resonates for you, but know this guidance is so real. It is constantly steering you in the right direction.

When you listen to that guidance, you feel at peace.

If you do not feel at peace, you are listening to another voice, one outside yourself or with a voice from your past or future.

The Master

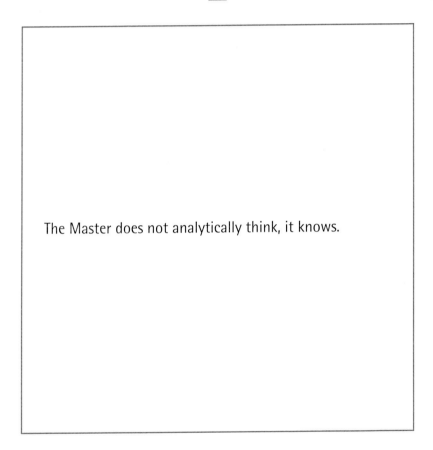

The Master does not analytically think, it knows.

Inner Knowing

How can you trust that you are hearing or sensing the right voice, your inner knowing?

First you must trust that this is within you. A golden compass guiding you, it's called your soul. A constant navigational system.

Going in the right direction, you simply will feel better. You are aligned to your soul. Journeying in the wrong direction, the more out of sync you will feel with your own soul. Your body will not feel at ease.

Soul Catcher

Constant

Your soul is the highest intelligence and the one that is reliable.

Your thoughts and emotions are not constant, they are ever fluctuating and your job is to line up with similar thoughts of your soul. Loving, peaceful, kind thoughts.

The Empty Cup

Know that your job is to let your mind go blank, to enter the silence within or become an empty cup in your mind. Only then true real guidance will come forth or maybe you will come into centre. When you are out of thought, this is your highest vibration; you are then allowing the fullness of who you are.

If the cup is full with clutter and distraction, you will not hear that inner voice. Your vibration becomes diluted. To become an empty cup; meditation, prayer, and nature is highly recommended to get you there.

The Master's Voice

Some people hear it, feel it or see it! Everyone is different but what everyone has in common is that it will feel amazing. It will feel right.

No matter what your head tells you, your feelings are your barometer! If you feel still and centered then you are right on track with your true self, your soul!

The highest intelligence!

Divine Intelligence

—

The master guides you and gives you messages, brings opportunities to you and everything you want and need. The master knows you more than you know yourself, consciously that is. You will see a divine intelligence working in your life, creating miracles if you tune into it.

Wait For The Impulse

Be like the cat waiting for the mouse

The mouse appears.

The cat catapults itself into action and catches the mouse.

It is the energy, the inner knowing, that directs when to go for it, the master within.

Receive

You are a receptacle like a telephone, or transmitter, receiving information. This information comes through the airwaves. You will only receive the message if you have picked up the phone – if you are connected.

Focus On What You Want

Just like searching the web, all the information is out there. Exactly what you type into your search engine is exactly the answer you will get back. Therefore ask good questions. Focus on positive stuff. Search for the good stuff and focus only on what you want.

Space

―

Create space inside your mind. Eliminate thinking of the past and future as much as possible. Spot the differences between the following pictures. Which one do you choose to emulate?

by Cara Pilbeam

Choice

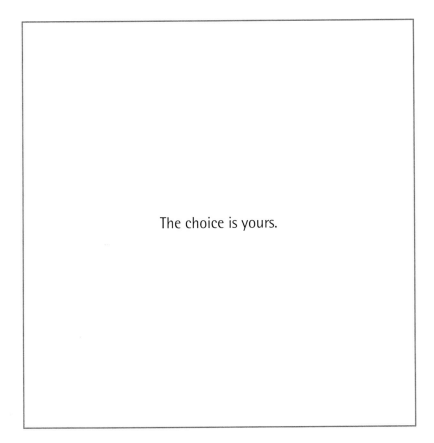

The choice is yours.

Present

See how you look and feel when you are just here in the present moment. Your worry lines will disappear. The now, is the most powerful peaceful place to be.

Mind Your Own Business

Whatever anyone thinks is none of your business. Whatever anyone thinks of you is also none of your business.

Journey

Every soul is on its own journey. You are only responsible, for your own individual one.

Light And Beauty

Whatever anyone thinks of you and says about you, is actually what they are saying about themselves. If they see light and beauty in you, it's because they already have seen that at some stage within themselves.

Night Falls

Night falls upon one so precious.

All your dreams float overhead

Wandering through,

The night-time sky.

The cosmic womb of every breath,

Creative thought,

Word and feeling.

The cosmic knowing of all in store

Who decides if you can soar?

It is only you, all of it is you.

Alchemy

The resting nature is all it takes

To pull those dreams from sky to earth.

Rest well dear one,

For now your dreams will become real,

Magical as they will be

You will know and see yourself,

as truth.

Love Is The Answer

Mirror, mirror on the wall, love is the greatest healer of them all.

Life

Falling in love is highly recommended...with yourself.
When you do, you fall in love with life.

Together

Love is embedded into every cell of your body. It is the glue that holds you together.

Peace

Inner peace is where? Inside of you.

Flowing

Stop fighting.
Start flowing.
When you start flowing,
You begin glowing.
When you are glowing,
You are now loving.

The Difference A Few Letters Can Make

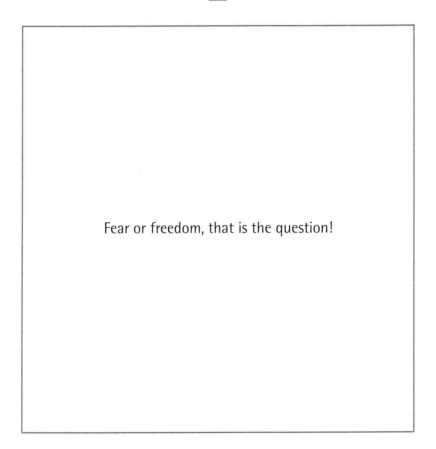

Fear or freedom, that is the question!

Flame

Light the flame within your own heart and that flame will not only keep you warm but cradle others just by your glowing presence.

Human Reset

Love is actually who you are.

Make it your default button.

Body

Love your entire body because your body is your vehicle which carries your soul.

Reason

If someone is not loving towards you, they have a very good reason. You have no idea what they are going through or have gone through in this lifetime or in others.

Ask

Helpful question to have in your pocket: ask yourself, how can I come from love here?

Even better if you remember yourself as love, then all will fall into place. Great things will flow to you when you are in that space.

Focus

Line up with the love, peace and Zen that already resides in you. Make this your number one priority as soon as you awake. Then during the day keep this as your number one focus, it will have far reaching benefits that will astonish you.

Align

It may take prayer or meditation or just consciously aligning yourself to this higher power first thing in the morning but it will be worth it.

Let Go Of The Struggle

Let go of the having to figure out the how, let go of when, let go of who, let go of making it happen, instead work with the universe intelligently. Know your place, know your job is to ask and the universe will give it onto you. The universe will figure out all the mechanics of it. You just ask for what you want, let it go by becoming the empty cup, allowing it to happen.

Peace

There is no right or wrong. When we accept reality, peace is assured.

Eye Of The Storm

You are lying there,

Dustbowls sweep across your mind at night,

As daylight turns to dusk.

You fear your aloneness.

This life fading, the soul longing.

This time feels like you have no belonging.

Visibility fades and light disappears.

No light anymore,

The night feels long and cold.

)

Eye of the Storm

———

When one becomes a foe onto oneself,

And no friend understands,

It's like a time where nobody knows.

Another day,

And now feeling more alone than ever before

This time will pass,

There is nothing for you to do,

It is sacred time,

A secret from

Me to you.

Feel It in Your Heart

Freedom is finding out that you are loved by this great unfathomable force, the non-physical aspect. It is constantly loving and supporting you. Feel that in your heart.

Raw Honesty

Be honest with yourself at all times about how you are feeling. Give yourself permission to take off the mask and be real. It's okay to be down, up and inside out, it's called your emotions. Children are excellent at feeling their emotions, they express them, so should you.

Fun

If you spend time doing what you love, then you will love what you do and what you do will not feel like work. It will feel like fun.

Get Centered

Don't act or react until first you get yourself into a loving space. When you are anchored there, you can set sail. The right course will come forth, it will be clear.

Sometimes it might take standing beside a tree, or being barefoot in the garden to allow yourself get grounded and centered. This will clear your mind and ensure you are making decisions from a clear and balanced place.

"We should be having epiphanies every day."

Yolanda Barker – Filmmaker

Gifts

Love and appreciate the gifts you have been given. Everyone has at least one gift if not plenty more. If you don't recognise your gifts, then no one else will.

Activate

Ignite your dormant gifts, many more lay waiting to be activated.

Pain

Pain is here,

Pain is real,

It is true

No matter what they say.

How can I escape?

How can I be free?

It's not possible

I hear you say.

You try to run,

You try to hide,

But will you stop for goodness sake.

〉

I am the divine,

Trying to communicate

The very thing you want to placate.

What, you are the divine?

Well how can there be so much pain?

Because my child,

You simply forget,

I am here always, never fret.

〉

Always here but how, you cannot be.

I am fumbling, I am meek and I hurt.

Yes my child you do,

But it is only because

You do not truly know your worth.

Cook

When you bake or cook, always remember one of the important ingredients...LOVE.

Sprinkle it in before you serve. It will taste so different.

Become Like The River

I am a river.

Constantly flowing

Choosing the path of least resistance

Allowing myself to glide over stones

Never ceasing.

If I run dry

I trust

I know the rains will come

Replenish me.

⟩

Constantly flowing and allowing,

Never ceasing

Joining with the huge ocean.

I am one with it.

The same water that is in the rain

Is the same in the river

As in the ocean,

No separation.

Life cannot stop.

Become like the river,

Let me guide you

To the wisdom I hold.

Peace

Inner peace is always here within you. Find the pattern of thought that is taking you away from the Zen that is already inside of you.

See you don't have to find inner peace. You just have to find out what you are thinking that is creating non peace. Identify that and change those thoughts to loving ones for yourself. Immediately you will line up again with your true divine nature.

Reality

How amazing is it that each of us get to choose our own reality. Whatever you think about yourself is entirely up to you.

Constant

—

Your inner being is a constant, a light that is always on. A light burning so brightly, a voice calling you home in every heartbeat. You are either at home in yourself or you have wandered off the path.

Divine

The one constant is the divine within. Divine love is present in every human heart. Sometimes the wounds of life cover this up but all the same it is in there, in every single human being. Find it within yourself and you will see it in others.

Feelings

Allow yourself to feel your feelings. Just feel. If you want to run away from the feeling and avoid feeling it, breathe into it. Feel, and that allows the energy to flow. If you find your mind is very busy, you are avoiding dropping down into your feelings.

Do not go into a story in your mind. Stay down, breathe, feel and when you feel peace or relief in your body, you know you have moved the energy. Well done!

Real Self

To sometimes understand why you move away from your real self or you lose yourself, it is because you are feeling less than. You feel unworthy. Tell yourself you are worthy and your self worth will become so worthwhile as you reap the enormous benefits of worthiness.

Guilt

Give up the guilt. Guilt is a stinky emotion. It is not based on the present moment. It's based on the past. The present moment is actually all that is real.

Fingertips

You've not only got the whole world in your hands, you have got the entire universe. Your fingertips are your magic wands, use them wisely.

Magic

There is black magic and white magic. Either one is created with the words you use or the thoughts you have. Good or bad. Be dedicated to pure magic and leave a trail of starlight behind you.

Silence

Everything miraculous grows out of silence. Think about it. A baby in a woman's womb, a tree from the soil, a flower, even an invention. All these started as seeds to become the thing they were destined to be.

Vibrations

There are many vibrations, good, bad, high and low ones, but the only vibration you should concern yourself with is the one of source, the one that calls your inner name. Your inner being, your true self, your true north.

The great news is you only have control over this one. You have no control over other people's vibrations or the world around you. Give up trying to control things you cannot control. Instead focus on your inner alignment to filling your inner well. Make it paradise.

It's A State of Mind

Heaven and hell are real. I have experienced them both and that was just yesterday.

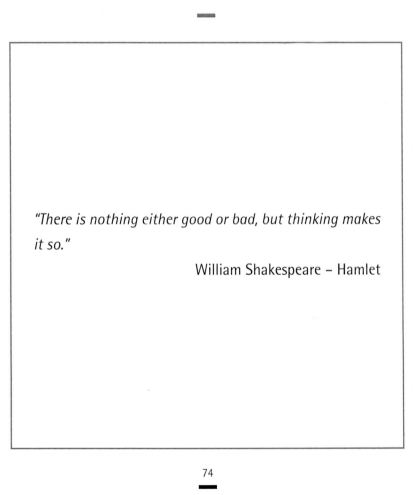

"There is nothing either good or bad, but thinking makes it so."

William Shakespeare – Hamlet

The Choice

The good news is, you have a choice to choose one or the other, heaven or hell. The great news is you can choose one or the other in every minute. You don't have to stay in inner turmoil for days or hours, remember you have the control. The choice.

Limbo

Sometimes Limbo is an option, that inbetween place of waiting and not knowing. Honour that space because great change happens underneath the surface and be gentle on yourself if you are unsure and don't know anything. It's okay to not know at times. Your inner being is taking care of it all, of you. Trust. It knows even if you don't.

Trust

Trust is underrated. If we are trusting life, we have peace, if we are not, we are on shaky ground.

Designed, typeset, printed and bound in Ireland by

PubliBook Ireland
www.publibookireland.com